quick & easy
Family
Dinners

Gooseberry Patch Cookbooks...
they're homemade...
made easy!

Gooseberry Patch cookbooks are all about
friends sharing recipes with friends.

The recipes are easy! They use ingredients
that you have in the pantry, they're
yummy and they help you get
dinner on the table...fast.

Check out our newest titles
or start your collection today at
www.gooseberrypatch.com/cookbooks

Barbecued Honey Ham

1 c. French honey-style salad
   dressing
1 c. catsup
1 c. apple butter

1/2 c. steak sauce
1 T. Worcestershire sauce
2 lbs. cooked ham, sliced
12 hamburger buns, split

In a large bowl combine all ingredients except ham and buns.
Place ham into an ungreased 13"x9" casserole dish. Pour sauce
over ham. Bake at 350 degrees for 30 minutes. Serve on buns.
Makes 6 servings.

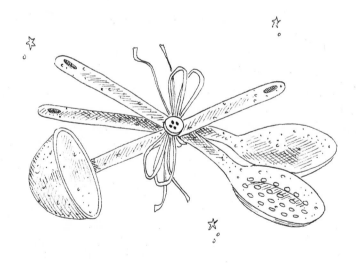

For a really quick side dish, cook chopped green peppers
in butter for about 5 minutes. Add canned corn and
salt and simmer until golden...yummy!

Mom's Potato Salad

5 lbs. red potatoes, peeled,
    cooked and diced
1 doz. eggs, hardboiled,
    peeled and diced
3 T. sugar
3 T. mustard

3 T. horseradish sauce
5 T. dill pickle juice
Optional: yellow food
    coloring
32-oz. jar mayonnaise
1 onion, chopped

Combine potatoes and eggs in a bowl. Mix remaining
ingredients together. Pour over the potatoes and eggs; mix well.
Refrigerate a few hours before serving. Serves 15.

*If you find time is too short to make your own potato
salad dressing, bottled coleslaw dressing is a great-tasting
substitute. Add as much of the dressing as you like to
potato salad ingredients, then stir gently to blend.*

Oven-Fried Chicken

1 egg, beaten
1/2 c. milk
1 c. all-purpose flour
2 T. chopped pecans
1 t. baking powder
2 t. salt
2 T. sesame seed
2-1/2 to 3 lbs. chicken,
   quartered
1/4 lb. butter, melted

In a medium bowl, combine egg and milk. In a separate bowl, mix together flour, pecans, baking powder, salt and sesame seed. Dip chicken in egg mixture, then in flour mixture, coating well. Drizzle with butter and place skin-side up on a baking sheet. Bake at 400 degrees for 30 minutes. Turn chicken, and cook until tender and golden. Makes 4 servings.

Mmm...mashed potatoes are the ultimate comfort food.
Simmer potatoes in chicken broth instead of water
for delicious flavor.

★ *quick & easy* family dinners ★

Quick Pizza Mac

1-1/2 c. elbow macaroni,
    cooked
8-oz. jar pizza sauce
8-oz. container cottage
    cheese

4-oz. pkg. sliced pepperoni,
    halved
1/2 c. onion, chopped
1/2 t. dried basil
1 T. grated Parmesan cheese

In a lightly greased 2-quart casserole dish, combine all
ingredients except Parmesan cheese; blend well. Sprinkle
Parmesan over top. Cover; bake at 350 degrees for 30 to
35 minutes, or until heated through. Serves 6.

What a time-saver! Most casseroles can be prepared
the night before...just cover and refrigerate. Simply
add 15 to 20 minutes to the original baking time.

Judy's Pizza Rolls

1 lb. ground beef
1 onion, chopped
1 clove garlic, minced
8-oz. can pizza sauce
dried oregano and basil to
    taste

2/3 c. mozzarella cheese,
    cubed
8 hot dog buns, split

Sauté ground beef, onion and garlic in a skillet over medium heat; drain. Add pizza sauce, oregano and basil; lower heat and simmer for 30 minutes. Let cool slightly; stir in cheese. Fill buns with meat mixture; wrap individually in aluminum foil. Place on a baking sheet and bake at 425 degrees for 20 minutes. Serves 8.

Oh-so-easy iced tea...fill up a 2-quart pitcher with water
and drop in 6 to 8 teabags. Refrigerate overnight.
Discard teabags and add ice cubes and sugar
to taste...cool and refreshing!

Summertime Salad

2/3 c. vegetable or olive oil
1/2 t. salt
1 garlic clove, minced
pepper to taste
1/4 c. salad vinegar
3 T. fresh basil, chopped

1/4 c. onion, chopped
1-1/2 c. mozzarella cheese
   cubes
1 pt. cherry tomatoes,
   halved

Prepare dressing by mixing oil, salt, garlic, pepper and vinegar; toss in remaining ingredients. Chill until ready to serve. Serves 4.

If you stew a chicken to use later in chicken salads or casseroles, let it cool in its broth before cutting it into chunks...it will have twice the flavor.

Seashell Salad

2 c. shell macaroni, cooked
2 T. onion, chopped
1 c. salad shrimp, cooked
3 celery stalks, chopped
1-1/2 c. carrots, peeled and
    grated
2 c. frozen peas

1 t. salt
1/4 t. garlic powder
3/4 c. mayonnaise-style
    salad dressing
1/2 c. French salad dressing
Garnish: shoestring potatoes

Combine all ingredients except dressings and garnish; toss well. In a small bowl, combine mayonnaise-style salad dressing and French salad dressings; blend well and toss with salad. Garnish with shoestring potatoes. Serves 4 to 6.

For a side dish that practically cooks itself, fill aluminum foil
packets with sliced fresh veggies. Top with seasoning
salt and 2 ice cubes, seal and bake at 450 degrees
for 20 to 25 minutes. Delicious!

★ *quick & easy* family dinners ★

Ham-It-Up Casserole

16-oz. pkg. frozen French
   fries
16-oz. pkg. frozen chopped
   broccoli, cooked
1-1/2 c. cooked ham, cubed

10-3/4 oz. can cream of
   mushroom soup
1-1/4 c. milk
1/4 c. mayonnaise
1 c. grated Parmesan cheese

Arrange fries in a greased 13"x9" baking pan. Top with
broccoli; sprinkle with ham and set aside. Combine soup, milk
and mayonnaise in a small bowl; mix well and pour evenly
over ham. Sprinkle with cheese. Bake, uncovered, at
375 degrees for 40 minutes. Serves 4 to 6.

A crisp green salad goes well with all kinds of comforting
main dishes. For a zippy lemon dressing, shake up 1/2 cup
olive oil, 1/3 cup fresh lemon juice and a tablespoon of
Dijon mustard in a small jar and chill to blend.

Super-Easy Stuffed Peppers

4 green peppers, tops
   removed
1 lb. ground beef
1 onion, diced
3 T. Italian seasoning
1 clove garlic, pressed

3 c. prepared rice
26-oz. can spaghetti sauce,
   divided
salt and pepper to taste
Garnish: grated Parmesan
   cheese

Bring a large saucepan of water to a boil; add peppers and boil
until tender. Drain and set aside. Brown ground beef with onion
in a skillet; drain. Add Italian seasoning and garlic. Combine
ground beef mixture, prepared rice and all except 1/2 cup
spaghetti sauce in a large bowl. Add salt and pepper to taste.
Arrange peppers in a lightly greased 8"x8" baking pan. Fill
peppers completely with ground beef mixture, spooning any
extra mixture between peppers. Top with reserved sauce.
Lightly cover with aluminum foil; bake at 400 degrees for 30 to
45 minutes. Sprinkle with Parmesan cheese. Serves 4.

Serving salad alongside dinner tonight? Tear greens and
place in a large plastic bowl with a tight-fitting lid.
Add any favorite salad toppers and dressing,
then tighten the lid and shake to toss.

1-2-3 Cake

20-oz. can crushed pineapple
21-oz. can cherry pie filling
18-1/2 oz. yellow cake mix,
    divided

1 c. chopped walnuts *or pecans*
1 c. margarine, sliced

Place pineapple with juice in an ungreased 13"x9" baking dish; spread pie filling evenly over the top. Sprinkle with half of the cake mix, then with nuts. Sprinkle with remaining cake mix; dot margarine over top. Bake at 350 degrees for one hour. Serves 8 to 10.

Cut cake into cubes and layer in parfait glasses with
pudding, fruit or ice cream...a tasty dessert
just like Mom used to make.

Cherry Delight

2 c. graham cracker crumbs
4 T. sugar
4 T. butter, melted
2 8-oz. pkgs. cream cheese, softened

2 eggs, slightly beaten
1 c. sugar
1 t. vanilla
8-oz. can cherry pie filling

Combine graham cracker crumbs, sugar and butter; press into a lightly oiled 13"x9" baking dish. Beat cream cheese, eggs, sugar and vanilla together until fluffy and pour into crust. Bake at 350 degrees for 15 to 20 minutes until set. Cool for 2 hours. When completely cooled, top with pie filling. Serves 10 to 12.

When whisking ingredients in a bowl, a damp kitchen towel can keep them mixing bowl in place. Just twist the towel securely around the base of the bowl.

Peach Crinkle

29-oz. can sliced peaches,
    drained
1 t. lemon zest
1-1/4 c. pie crust mix
3/4 c. brown sugar, packed

2 T. butter
Garnish: whipped topping or
    ice cream

Place peaches in an ungreased 8"x8" baking pan. Add lemon zest. Crumble pie crust mix and brown sugar together, mix well. Sprinkle brown sugar mixture evenly over peaches and dot with butter. Bake at 350 degrees for 45 minutes. Serve warm with whipped topping or ice cream. Makes 8 to 10 servings.

Enjoy leftover slices of pie or cobbler by heating them
in the microwave on high for about 10 seconds. Top
servings with a big scoop of ice cream and
drizzle of honey for a yummy dessert.

Prize-Winning Chocolate Chip Cookies

3 c. all-purpose flour
1 t. baking soda
1-1/2 t. salt
1 c. margarine
1-1/3 c. sugar

2/3 c. brown sugar, packed
2 t. vanilla extract
2 eggs, beaten
3 c. semi-sweet chocolate
  chips

Combine flour, baking soda and salt; set aside. Cream margarine and sugars in a large mixing bowl; blend in vanilla and eggs until smooth. Gradually mix in dry ingredients; fold in chocolate chips. Drop by heaping tablespoonfuls about 3 inches apart onto parchment paper-lined baking sheets; bake at 325 degrees for 10 to 12 minutes. Makes about 4 dozen.

Make a game of table talk! Write fun questions on file cards...what kind of animal would you like to be? What's your favorite book? and so on. Pull a different card each night to talk about.

Golden Cheddar Biscuits

1/4 c. shortening
1 t. sugar
1 c. all-purpose flour
2 t. baking powder
1/4 t. salt

1 t. garlic powder
1 egg, beaten
1/3 c. milk
1 c. Cheddar cheese, grated

Cream shortening and sugar. Mix dry ingredients together; add to shortening and sugar mixture. Blend in remaining ingredients. Divide mixture equally into greased muffin cups. Bake at 400 degrees for 20 minutes, or until golden. Makes one dozen.

Oops, you got carried away and brought home too many fresh veggies from the farmers' market! Save them by cooking up a big pot of soup or stew and freezing it in meal-size portions.

Oven Beef & Noodles

1-1/2 oz. pkg. onion soup
    mix
4 c. water
10-3/4 oz. can cream of
    mushroom soup

3-lb. boneless beef chuck
    roast
12-oz. pkg. kluski egg
    noodles, uncooked
2 T. dried parsley

Combine onion soup mix and water in a covered roasting pan; stir in mushroom soup. Place roast in pan on top of soup mixture. Cover and bake at 350 degrees for 4 hours, or until meat is very tender. Remove roast from pan and shred; return to pan. Add noodles to pan; reduce heat to 300 degrees and bake for 20 to 30 minutes, checking and stirring every 15 minutes until noodles are tender. Add water if necessary to prevent drying out. Sprinkle with parsley before serving. Makes 6 to 8 servings.

Whip up a cool fruit dessert...you won't believe how easy
it is. Freeze an unopened can of your favorite fruit.
At serving time, scoop out frozen fruit and
process in a food processor until smooth.

Country Meatloaf

1-1/2 lbs. ground beef
1 c. herb-flavored stuffing
   mix
10-3/4 oz. can cream of
   mushroom soup, divided

1 egg, beaten
1/2 onion, chopped
2 T. sour cream

Combine ground beef, stuffing mix, half the soup, egg and onion; spread in an ungreased 9"x5" loaf pan. Bake at 400 degrees for 35 minutes. Mix remaining soup with sour cream; spread over meatloaf. Bake for an additional 5 to 10 minutes. Serves 3 to 4.

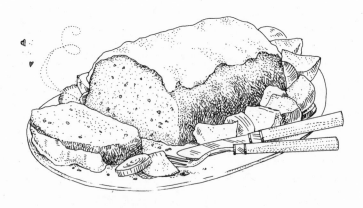

A quick & easy side dish...quarter new potatoes and toss with a little olive oil, salt and pepper. Spread on a baking sheet and bake at 400 degrees until crisp and golden, 35 to 40 minutes.

Slow-Cooker Savory Chicken Sandwiches

4 boneless, skinless chicken
   breasts
1-1/2 oz. pkg. onion soup
   mix
1/4 t. garlic salt
1/4 c. Italian salad dressing
1/4 c. water
4 sandwich buns, split
Garnish: lettuce, sliced
   cheese, sour cream or
   ranch salad dressing

Place chicken in a slow cooker; sprinkle with soup mix and
garlic salt. Pour dressing and water over chicken. Cover and
cook on low setting for 8 to 9 hours. Remove chicken and
shred with 2 forks; return to slow cooker. Serve with a slotted
spoon on buns; garnish as desired. Makes 4 sandwiches.

Bags of shredded lettuce make quick work of recipes.
Keep a bag on hand not only for crispy tossed salads,
but for layered dips, sandwiches and wraps.

Twice-Baked Potato Casserole

6 potatoes, baked, cubed and
    divided
salt and pepper to taste
1 lb. bacon, crisply cooked,
    crumbled and divided
3 c. sour cream, divided
8-oz. pkg. shredded
    mozzarella cheese,
    divided

8-oz. pkg. shredded Cheddar
    cheese, divided
Garnish: 2 green onions,
    chopped

Place half of cubed potatoes in a greased 13"x9" baking pan;
sprinkle with salt and pepper. Top with half each of bacon, sour
cream and cheeses; repeat layers. Bake for 350 degrees for
20 minutes. Sprinkle with green onions before serving.
Serves 8.

Use Mom's vintage baking dishes from the 1950's to
serve up casseroles with sweet memories. If you don't have
any of hers, keep an eye open at tag sales and thrift stores...
you may find the very same kind of dishes she used!

Creamy Macaroni & Cheese

6 T. butter, divided
3 T. all-purpose flour
2 c. milk
8-oz. pkg. cream cheese,
  cubed
2 c. Cheddar cheese,
  shredded

2 t. spicy brown mustard
1/2 t. salt
1/4 t. pepper
7-oz. pkg. elbow macaroni,
  cooked
3/4 c. bread crumbs
2 T. fresh parsley, minced

Melt 4 tablespoons butter in a large saucepan. Stir in flour until
smooth. Gradually add milk; bring to a boil. Cook and stir for
2 minutes. Reduce heat, add cheeses, mustard, salt and
pepper. Stir until cheese is melted and sauce is smooth. Add
macaroni to cheese sauce; stir to coat. Transfer to a lightly
greased 3-quart baking dish. In a separate saucepan, melt
the remaining butter and toss with bread crumbs and parsley;
sprinkle over macaroni. Bake, uncovered, at 400 degrees for
15 to 20 minutes or until golden. Makes 6 to 8 servings.

Try using a different shape of pasta next time you make
macaroni & cheese. Wagon wheels, seashells and bowties
all hold cheese sauce well...they're fun for kids too!

★ *quick & easy* family dinners ★

Sloppy Joes

1 lb. ground beef	1 t. sugar
10-3/4 oz. can tomato soup	1 sm. onion, diced
1/2 green pepper, diced	2 T. Worcestershire sauce
2 T. vinegar	4 to 6 sandwich buns, split

Brown ground beef in a medium saucepan and drain. Add remaining ingredients to beef and stir. Simmer on low heat for 30 to 60 minutes, until heated through. Serve on buns. Serves 4 to 6.

Turn leftover Sloppy Joe sauce into a tasty quick casserole...
spread it in a baking pan, top with cheese slices and
refrigerated biscuits. Bake until bubbly and
biscuits are golden.

Homestyle Baked Spaghetti

8-oz. pkg. cream cheese,
   softened
1-1/2 c. sour cream
2 to 3 T. onion, grated
12-oz. pkg. fine egg noodles,
   cooked
2 lbs. ground beef, browned

2 t. salt
3 6-oz. cans tomato paste
2 c. water
2 t. sugar
1 t. pepper
Garnish: grated Parmesan
   cheese

Blend cream cheese, sour cream and onion; stir in cooked
noodles. Place in bottom of 3-quart casserole dish; set aside.
Combine remaining ingredients except garnish in a saucepan;
heat thoroughly. Pour over noodles; sprinkle with Parmesan
cheese. Bake at 350 degrees for 45 minutes. Serves 8.

Garlic-Cheese Bread

3-1/2 c. biscuit baking mix
2-3/4 c. shredded Cheddar
   cheese

1 t. garlic powder
1-1/4 c. milk
2 eggs, beaten

Combine all ingredients until just moistened; spread evenly into
a greased 9"x5" loaf pan. Bake at 350 degrees for 30 to
40 minutes; cool on wire rack. Makes 8 servings.

*Whip up a tasty dip for sliced fruit. Swirl fruit preserves
into vanilla yogurt... just the thing for hungry kids
waiting for dinnertime.*

Confetti Coleslaw

6 c. cabbage, shredded
1 c. red cabbage, shredded
1 carrot, peeled and
    shredded
1/2 red pepper, cut into strips
1/4 c. sweet onion, chopped
3/4 c. mayonnaise-type
    salad dressing Miracle
          Whip

2 T. lime juice or Vinegar
1 T. fresh dill, snipped
1-1/2 t. sugar
1/4 t. salt
1/4 t. pepper

Combine cabbage, carrot, red pepper and onion in a large bowl; set aside. Blend remaining ingredients together in a small bowl; mix well. Pour over cabbage mixture; toss to coat. Cover and chill for at least 2 hours; stir before serving. Serves 8 to 10.

Making a casserole for a small family? Divide the casserole ingredients into two small dishes and freeze one for later. Casseroles that don't freeze well can be shared with a friend or neighbor.

Tangy Glazed Carrots

1 lb. carrots, peeled and
    cooked
3 T. butter, melted

2 T. brown sugar
1 T. Dijon mustard
1/2 t. ground ginger

Place carrots in a bowl, set aside. Whisk together remaining ingredients and pour over carrots. Toss gently. Makes 6 servings.

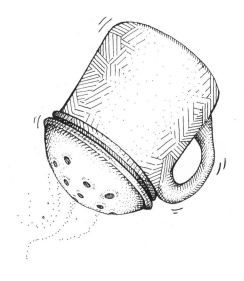

Fill a big shaker with a favorite all-purpose spice mixture...
keep it by the stove for a dash of flavor on
meats and veggies as they cook.

Fiesta Beef Soup

1 lb. ground beef
15-oz. can ranch-style
   beans, drained
14-1/2 oz. can tomatoes
   with chiles

11-oz. can corn with diced
   peppers, drained
1-1/4 oz. pkg. taco
   seasoning mix

Brown ground beef in a stockpot; drain. Stir in remaining ingredients; lower heat and simmer for 15 to 20 minutes until heated through. Serves 6 to 8.

Declare a Picnic Night at home! Just toss a checkered tablecloth on the dinner table and set out paper plates and disposable plastic utensils. Relax and enjoy dinner... no dishes to wash!

Slow-Cooker Taco Soup

1 lb. ground beef
1 onion, diced
1 clove garlic, minced
12-oz. bottle green taco
   sauce
4-oz. can green chiles
2 to 3 15-oz. cans black
   beans, drained and
   rinsed

15-1/4 oz. can corn, drained
15-oz. can tomato sauce
2 c. water
1-1/4 oz. pkg. taco
   seasoning mix
Garnish: sour cream,
   shredded Cheddar
   cheese, corn chips

Brown beef, onion and garlic in a large skillet over medium heat; drain. In a slow cooker, combine beef mixture and remaining ingredients except garnish. Cover and cook on high setting for one hour. Serve with sour cream, shredded cheese and corn chips. Serves 8 to 10.

A spicy side in no time. Heat a 16-ounce bag of frozen corn in one teaspoon oil for 5 to 10 minutes. Stir in a 7-oz. jar of roasted red chiles, finely diced and one teaspoon each of cumin, chili powder, finely diced serrano chile and salt to taste. Heat through for 5 minutes...olé!

Sunny Day Brownies

2 c. all-purpose flour
1/4 t. baking soda
1 t. baking powder
3/4 t. salt
2/3 c. butter, melted
2 c. brown sugar, packed

2 eggs, beaten
2 t. vanilla extract
1 c. mini milk chocolate
  chips
3/4 c. chopped walnuts

Combine flour, baking soda, baking powder and salt in a large mixing bowl; set aside. In a separate bowl, blend butter and brown sugar together; mix in eggs and vanilla. Add flour mixture, stirring to blend. Spread batter into a lightly greased 13"x9" baking pan. Sprinkle with chocolate chips and nuts. Bake at 350 degrees for 30 minutes; cool in pan and cut into bars. Makes 12 to 15 bars.

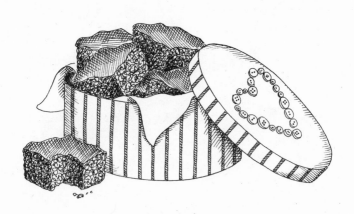

A real time-saver...double your sugar cookie recipe and freeze some of the dough in individual plastic bags. Thaw and bake for a quick, homemade treat.

Crustless Apple Pie

5 apples, cored, peeled and
   sliced
1 t. cinnamon
1 c. plus 1 T. sugar, divided

3/4 c. margarine, melted
1 c. all-purpose flour
1 egg, beaten

Place apples in a greased 2-quart casserole dish; sprinkle
with cinnamon and one tablespoon sugar. Mix remaining
ingredients; spread over apples. Bake at 350 degrees for 50 to
60 minutes. Serves 6 to 8.

An easy way to core apples and peaches...slice fruit in half
and then use a melon baller to scoop out the core.

Keep these basic pantry items on hand & you can whip up just about anything!

Bulk Items:
Biscuit & Pancake Mix
Brown Sugar
Dry Beans
Flour
Oats
Pasta
Rice
Sugar

Baking Items:
Baking Soda
Baking Powder
Baking Cocoa
Corn Syrup
Extracts & Flavorings
Salt

Spices & Herbs:
Basil
Bay Leaves
Chili Powder
Cinnamon
Garlic Powder
Dry Mustard
Nutmeg
Onion Flakes
Rosemary
Sage
Thyme

Canned items:
Creamed Soups
Diced Tomatoes
Fruits
Jams & Jellies
Tomato Paste

Canned Items, Cont.
Tomato Sauce
Vegetables
Whole Tomatoes

Condiments:
Barbeque Sauce
Bouillion Cubes
Catsup
Lemon Juice
Mayonnaise
Mustard
Salad Dressing
Soy Sauce
Vinegar
Worcestershire sauce

INDEX

*Enjoy these favorites from our **Gooseberry Patch** hardcover books!*

Did you *know?*

Gooseberry Patch has everything you need to make your house a cozy home!

- our very own line of cookbooks, calendars & organizers
- charming kitchenware like mixing bowls, cake stands & enamelware
- delicious gourmet goodies

- farmhouse, cottage, retro and primitive styles
- soft-as-a-feather handmade quilts
- night lights for every season

Call us toll-free at 1-800-854-6673, and we'd be delighted to send you our new catalog!

Or, shop with us online anytime at www.gooseberrypatch.com.

Send us your favorite recipe!

and the memory that makes it special for you!* If we select your recipe for a brand-new **Gooseberry Patch** cookbook, your name will appear right along with it...and you'll receive a FREE copy of the book! Submit your recipe on our website at **www.gooseberrypatch.com** or mail it to:

**Gooseberry Patch
Attn: Cookbook Dept.
P.O. Box 190
Delaware, OH 43015**

*Please include the number of servings and all other necessary information!